Hide and seek

By Jenny Giles

Illustrated by Elspeth Lacey

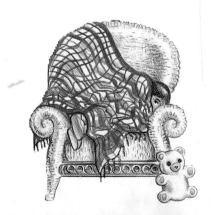

Dad said,

"**1** and **2** and **3** and . . . "

James hid in the box.

Dad said,

"**4** and **5** and **6** and . . . "

Nick hid on the chair.

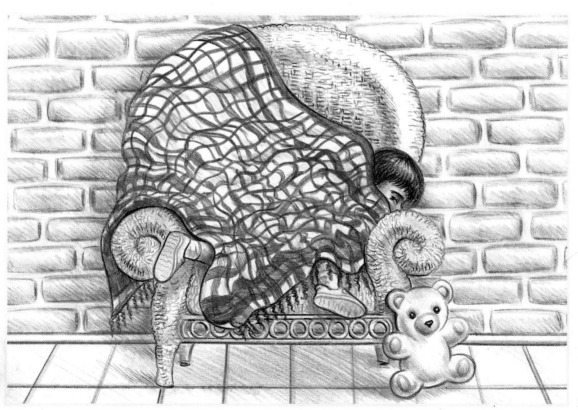

5

Dad said,

"**7** and **8** and **9** and . . . "

Kate hid up in the tree.

"**10!**" shouted Dad.
"Here I come!"

Dad looked in the box.
"I can see you, James,"
he said.

Dad looked at the chair. "I can see you, Nick," said Dad.

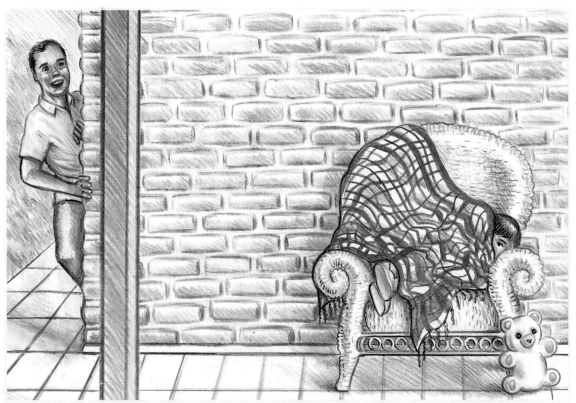

Dad looked for Kate.
He looked and looked
and **looked**.

"Where is Kate?" said Dad.
"Where is Kate?"

"Come here, Kate.
You win!" shouted Dad.
"Where **are** you?"

"Look in the tree, Dad,"
said Kate.

"Here I am!"